Dolphin, Fox, Hippo, and Ox

Mammal:

An animal that has fur or hair and drinks its mother's milk as a baby

Dolphin, Fox, Hippo, and Ox

What Is a Mammal?

by Brian P. Cleary

illustrations by Martin Goneau

M Millbrook Press • Minneapolis

A **mammal** is an animal with quite distinctive features

BIRDS

MAMMALS

FUR

MAKES MILK FOR BABIES

REPTILES

MAMMAL
SKULL

that make it very different
from a host of other creatures.

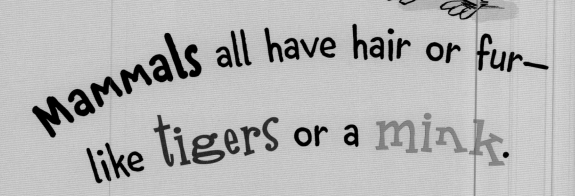

Mammals all have hair or fur—
like tigers or a mink.

6

And when they're very young,
their mothers' milk
is what they drink.

Before the day
they're born,

most **mammals** grow
inside their mamas

as in the case of cats and dogs,

lemurs, lambs, and llamas.

And what about the lion, leopard,

panther, panda, fox?

They're **mammals** like the porcupine,

the porpoise, pig, and ox!

Same with all the **hippos,**

hamsters, hedgehogs, hares, and camels.

Squirrels, skunks, and gerbils, rats?

You guessed it right—
they're **mammals!**

Some, like bats,
can fly through air,

and whales can swim the sea.

14

Other **mammals**
live on land—
the ones like you
and me!

They may eat meat or plants or both, use wings or arms and legs,

but nearly every **mammal** is born live, and not from eggs.

NURSERY

One egg-laying **mammal**
is the **platypus** female,

who warms her tiny eggs between her tummy and her tail.

Mammals all need air to breathe— that's why they all have lungs.

They also have three different kinds of teeth around their tongues.

Some teeth snip, and others pierce.
Some crush food
for what follows:

sending it from mouth to throat each time the **mammal** swallows.

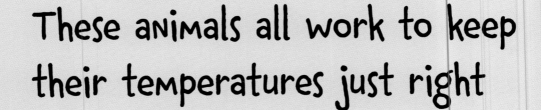

These animals all work to keep their temperatures just right

by making their own body heat

throughout the day and night.

Some have feet,

some have wings,

a few have spouts and fins.

Some have lots of fur
that covers
torso, arms, and shins.

These include chinchillas,

cheetahs,

chimpanzees

and boars,

elephants and otters, mice and moose, and many more!

boo!

So what is a **mammal?**
Do you know?

An animal is a mammal if . . .
- as a baby, it drinks milk from its mother;
- it has fur or hair. (The hair can be all over its body or just a little on one part of the body.)

In addition, all mammals . . .

- breathe air;
- look like their parents as babies (in an approximate sort of way);
- are warm-blooded. (That means they make their own body heat, so their bodies' temperature always stays about the same.)

And most mammals . . .

- grow inside their mothers' bodies;
- are born live. (Just a few mammals lay eggs.)

Find activities, games, and more at
www.brianpcleary.com

ABOUT THE AUTHOR & ILLUSTRATOR

BRIAN P. CLEARY is the author of the Words Are CATegorical®, Math Is CATegorical®, Adventures in Memory™, Sounds Like Reading®, and Food Is CATegorical™ series, as well as several picture books and poetry books. He lives in Cleveland, Ohio.

MARTIN GONEAU is the illustrator of the Food Is CATegorical™ series. He lives in Trois-Rivières, Québec.

LERNER e SOURCE™

Expand learning beyond this printed book. Download free, complementary educational resources for this book from our website, www.lernersource.com.

Text copyright © 2013 by Brian P. Cleary
Illustrations copyright © 2013 by Lerner Publishing Group, Inc.

Millbrook Press
A division of Lerner Publishing Group, Inc.
241 First Avenue North
Minneapolis, MN 55401 U.S.A.

Website address: www.lernerbooks.com

Tiger Fur Background: © Witr/Dreamstime.com.

Main body text set in Chauncy Decaf Medium 35/44. Typeface provided by the Chank Company.

Library of Congress Cataloging-in-Publication Data

Cleary, Brian P., 1959–
    Dolphin, Fox, Hippo, and Ox: What Is a Mammal? / by Brian P. Cleary ; illustrated by Martin Goneau.
       p.   cm. — (Animal groups are CATegorical)
    ISBN: 978-0-7613-6206-7 (lib. bdg. : alk. paper) 1. Mammals—Juvenile literature. I. Goneau, Martin, ill. II. Title.
  QL706.2.C54 2013
  599—dc23   2011044870
Sebco 02/18/13 19.95
Manufactured in the United States of America
1 – DP – 7/15/2012